D1477745

PHYSICAL EDUCATION IN PRIMARY SCHOOLS

General Editor : Margaret E. Anderson

Principal Lecturer in Physical Education
Hamilton College of Education

PHYSICAL EDUCATION IN PRIMARY SCHOOLS

Expressive

Movement

Elizabeth B. Murdoch

Senior Lecturer,
Dunfermline College
of Physical Education,
Edinburgh

W & R CHAMBERS
Edinburgh and London

Photographs: Alan Grant
Donald Millar

First published 1973

ISBN: 0 550 78803 4

Printed in Great Britain by
T & A Constable Ltd
Printers to the University of Edinburgh

CONTENTS

Part IV STAGES OF DEVELOPMENT

Part V ACCOMPANIMENT

Part VI LINKS WITH OTHER SUBJECTS

LIST OF PLATES

ACKNOWLEDGMENTS

The author and publishers wish to express their appreciation of the co-operation of Davidsons Mains Primary School, Cramond Primary School and Corstorphine Primary School, all Edinburgh, in making it possible to include the photographs and examples of creative writing.

The poem on page 82, *Cat* by Miss Eleanor Farjeon, is reproduced by kind permission of Michael Joseph and is taken from *Silver Sand and Snow.*

PREFACE

The Primary school curriculum has undergone many changes
in recent years and Physical Education has been subjected
to extensive rethinking. Now that we understand so much
more of the child's physical, mental and emotional growth,
it becomes possible to relate his physical activities to his stages
of development.

Expressive movement is an aspect of Physical Education
with which, until recently, the Primary school teacher has
been relatively unfamiliar. It suffered the reputation of being
somewhat amorphous, appearing to lack the structure evident
in the teaching of inventive movement and games skills. This
book is written to guide the teacher and the student in
training towards an awareness of the fundamental aspects
of expressive movement, i.e. dynamics, space patterns and
relationships.

As this awareness develops, teachers will be able to plan
their programme in expressive movement to the full advantage
of their pupils, ensuring progression in their experience and
learning. Only thus is it possible for the pupils' activities to
be educationally worth while.

Margaret E. Anderson

INTRODUCTION

Expressive Movement

Expressive movement

Expressive movement provides one way in which the child can learn more about his world. It gives him a particular understanding of it and of his place within it by affording him opportunity to respond to situations, and to make statements of his feelings and ideas. In order to achieve this he must become physically more skilful so that he can use his body as an expressive tool. Expressive movement lessons give the child a chance to explore and to enjoy movement.

Movement is a natural medium for children and does not rely on the written or spoken word for communication. Expressive movement should be approached not as a subject separated from others in any way but as a necessary part of a complete educational experience.

At first, the young child may be absorbed wholly in his own particular way of moving which has a significance known only to himself. As he gets older he becomes more interested in conveying his feelings and ideas to others. His increasing physical and intellectual skill enable him to do this more clearly. The latter allows him to think of what he wishes to express and also to choose the appropriate movements to do this. His physical ability allows him to be more successful in the movements of his choice and so makes his expression comparably clearer and more satisfying to himself and perhaps also to others.

Again, at this stage, he can become engrossed in movement for its own sake. He may for a time be caught up in a repetition of sensation which is, for him, totally absorbing. The child who turns round and round as he travels, rising and sinking gently and rhythmically in each revolution, is totally captured by this experience and it is for him, at that moment, complete. In this he learns something about himself and movement and he needs many such experiences to build a rich vocabulary of movement.

An expressive movement lesson provides the environment in which the child can meet with these experiences. He can leap for the sheer joy of leaping, or rush across the room to

8

1 Gentle turning

express the exhilaration of speed, or move in a slow, gentle way which conveys a calm, solemn mood. All this helps the child to objectify his feelings and so come to terms with them in a completely acceptable way, bringing him gradually to an understanding of movement as a means of expression.

'It is only fear that prevents the child from being an artist—fear that his private world of fantasy will seem ridiculous to the adult, fear that its expressive signs and symbols will not be adequate. Cast out fear from the child and you have then released all its potentialities for emotional growth and maturation.'*

Adult affirmation is essential if the child is going to expose his feelings, thoughts and ideas through movement, and it can be shown through acceptance of his youthful attempts in expressive movement lessons. In order to understand himself and his powers of expression, the child needs the positive support of lessons which capture his imagination and clearly guide him through each stage in the development of this understanding.

Expressive movement provides for children one means of answering the creative challenge to build and form their ideas into finished pieces of work. Some may find that their creative ability is fulfilled in the medium of paint, others in words or yet others in clay, but there will be some who have a greater affinity towards, and so a greater facility with, the medium of movement, which is therefore the best way for them to approach this challenge. Expressive movement lessons give these children the opportunity to work in a medium in which they may find themselves more fluent and more flexible than they could be in any other.

* *The Grass Roots of Art*, Sir Herbert Read (Faber)

PART I

Movement content

Movement content

It is important to recognise the particular movement characteristics of children. These are in no way pale shadows or
diminutions of adult movement. The movement world of
children is a place exclusively inhabited by them. Any attempt
to imprint adult standards, patterns or rhythms will be un-
successful. This may even be harmful to the natural development
of the children's movement ability. Thus we must observe
children moving.

When we do this we should be aware of four main aspects:

1 **Activities** which tell us *what* the children are doing.
2 **Dynamics** which tell us *how* the children are moving.
(Here we observe the rhythmical nature of
movement.)
3 **Space** which tells us *where* the children are moving.
4 **Relationships** which tell us *to what* the children are
relating their movement.

All four aspects can be observed in any movement. If we watch
a child swiftly swerving in and out as he threads his way among
his classmates, we may say that his *activity* is *travelling* about
the room; that the *dynamic* aspect is one of *speed*; that he is
moving through *space* with a rapid *change of direction* and that
the *relationship* he sets up is one of *avoiding* his classmates.

Activities

The basis of children's movement responses is seen in various
activities:

jumping: leaping; bounding; bouncing
turning: spinning; revolving; wheeling
travelling: running; skipping; sliding
stepping: tip-toeing; marching; creeping
gesture: bending; stretching; twisting; reaching
and
stillness: pausing; holding still; freezing

The children may combine any of these activities, e.g. hopping

13

is a combination of jumping and travelling when it takes the children across the floor. Stepping with a clearly defined action of stretching the leg before each step will bring about large steps and is a combination of stepping and gesture. Turning while in the air can be an exhilarating experience and is a combination of turning and jumping.

Dynamics

The dynamics of children's movement are mainly quick and slow, strong and light. The children may begin slowly then speed up, or quickly then slow down, or strongly then become more gentle, or lightly then become more vigorous. Some children naturally move quickly while others choose a slower tempo. Some whirl round or burst into the air with great strength while others drift gently round. Some enjoy deliberate, strong steps while others dart nimbly from place to place.

Unless otherwise guided by the teacher, the children may choose for themselves which of these variations they emphasise within their movement response but the teacher should ensure that a balanced range of dynamics is experienced by each child,

e.g.　'Let's *all* travel very quickly and nimbly then pause, and repeat this a few times.'

then,　'We are all going to turn round and round very fast and then freeze . . . and again.'

Stressing the dynamics in any movement gives it a much more expressive quality.
Rhythm is an interplay of strong and light movement and quick and slow movement. A rhythmical pattern of steps may be formed by combining some strongly accented steps with some of a lighter quality, some of the steps also being quicker than others.

A phrase of *travel, pause . . . travel, pause . . . and sink* is rhythmical when the travelling begins strongly and quickly and gradually comes to rest. The sinking movement may be slow and strong or else a *collapse* when it is quick and heavy.

A rhythmical pattern facilitates achievement and promotes understanding since it requires repetition. Children need and enjoy the sensation of repetition of an activity: *turn and turn*

14

and turn . . . A suggestion for a suitable finish, e.g. 'Can you freeze at the end of your turning?', produces a pattern if the phrase is repeated:
   turn and turn and turn and freeze . . . and again . . .
or *travel, pause . . . travel, pause . . . sink . . . rise . . .*
   travel, pause . . . travel, pause . . . collapse!

Children derive great pleasure from rhythmic phrasing. They can sustain repetition for much longer than an adult and so should not be curtailed in this. When they begin to lose concentration or their performance deteriorates, then the repetition should cease. This period of time varies from phrase to phrase, from child to child and from class to class.

Space

As the children move it can be seen whether they enjoy moving at a low level near the floor or whether they enjoy the sensation of 'defying' gravity. (A child who is confident will more easily move away from the floor.) They should be encouraged to experience both activities and so to change level frequently as they explore movement possibilities. The children also show whether they have a natural tendency to concentrate their attention on the area close to their body or whether they are willing to spread and reach and widen the whole body. Some children need the security of moving in the area immediate to their body; others are bolder and venture further into space. Thus one child may turn in a narrow, thin way while another may enjoy a large expansive turn. Some may jump so that they appear to pierce through the air while others seem to fill a large space as they bound into the air.

The children should be made aware that as they travel over the floor they are making pathways. The shapes of these often interest them and, as they become more experienced, they appreciate that pathways can also be drawn in the air.

Their growing conception of space means that the children become aware of direction in space, such as forward, backward or diagonal movement, and that it is by changing direction that pathways are shaped. They are also able to discern whether their pathways are formed from straight lines, curves or a combination of both.

Relationships

For some children, moving by themselves gives them satisfaction, while for others the need to have someone else with
whom to work and move is very strong. Some others may
prefer being together in groups, either leading the group or
in the equally necessary capacity of being influenced and
guided by the leader in the movement experience. The children
can learn much from working with and observing their
fellows in movement. Relationships, therefore, are evident
in working and moving with other people and also in the
children's concern about their immediate environment. An
awareness of the floor can be extremely significant in a
sinking movement, or the ceiling in a movement phrase in
which rising is emphasised. Travelling towards a focal point
in the room gives the travelling some purpose and expression.
Yet another aspect of relationship is that which exists between
one part of the moving body and another part. One foot
'chasing' the other foot gives significance to a jump. One
hand reaching away from the other hand results in a spreading
turn.

In each of the above examples, *relationship* can be described
by such phrases as meeting and parting, going around,
chasing and catching, avoiding and capturing, reaching
towards and away from. Emphasis on relationship gives
meaning to movement and thus it is an essential part of
expressive movement. The teacher should endeavour to give
her pupils experience in all of these aspects of relationship.

All of the children's natural tendencies in movement, as seen
under these four headings, form the basis of expressive movement and the content of expressive movement lessons.
The diagram on page 18 summarises the content.

ACTIVITIES

a Jumping
Turning
Travelling
Stepping
Gesture
Stillness

b Combinations:
Turning jumps
Turning while travelling
Travelling jumps
Stepping with gesture
Stepping turns

c Gesture of the whole body which results in the changing of the body's shape, e.g.

Stretching - thin or wide shaping

Bending - small, curled shaping

Twisting - screw-like shaping

DYNAMICS

a Strong
Light
Quick
Slow

b Becoming more gentle
Becoming more vigorous
Speeding up
Slowing down

c Rhythm
Rhythmic phrases

SPACE

a Changing levels:
high   medium   low

b Extension into space:
near to and far from

c Pathways
(i) on the floor
(ii) in the air

d Changing directions of movement

e Curved or straight lines

RELATIONSHIPS

a With a partner

b With a small group

c With a focus on the immediate environment

d Between two parts of the body

PART II

The lesson

The lesson

'... not into the child but from the child ...'*

In attempting to answer the question 'What is a good lesson form?', one is faced with two alternatives. The *first* is to recommend a format which one can follow for almost all lessons and, in so doing, to feel sure that a certain balance of experience has been given to the class. This format gives confidence in that it safeguards an order of events; it ensures that the lesson has a form and should be satisfying to the children because it culminates in a rich and complete experience.

The *second* arises from examining the nature of the subject. This means the setting up of a situation in which the children are given the opportunity to be creative, within the medium of movement, and to express what they think and feel. It follows that one cannot expect to anticipate and prepare for all possibilities as in the form and content of a planned lesson. The whole exchange remains open-ended and developments dictate form.

It is not possible to adopt or jettison either answer entirely. Both must be examined and a decision made as to which aspects of each will provide the best situation for both the class and the teacher. What must be remembered is that some measure of form is needed to ensure guided and recognisable progress, while at the same time there is a need for freedom to allow for individual, and indeed group, exploration and discovery. The balance between freedom and form is decided by the teacher and is dependent upon the experience and ability of the children.

Within a creative situation both children and teacher should contribute. The lesson should offer an opportunity for teacher's time and children's time. Initially, the teacher's time is devoted to presenting certain ideas and to setting up situations in which

* *Child Art,* W. Viola (University of London Press, 1962)

21

she knows that the children will all have the same experience, e.g. 'We will all turn slowly at first then get a little faster, then slower again.' She needs to guide many of the children's experiences in this way to ensure:

(a) that the children all have a common experience on which the teacher may build a developing idea;

(b) that the children have clear goals set and that the teacher can help them to reach them;

(c) that the children will be exposed to a variety of situations, some of which may be quite new to them.

The teacher must know which of the above she is attempting to achieve.

During the children's time in the lesson the children may explore the possibilities of a movement idea, either as individuals or in groups. In this way they may build their own movement phrases and perhaps create the culminating dance. Each individual or group must work at their own pace and refer to the teacher for guidance on improving or clarifying the performance. They involve her as audience: 'Look! Tell us what you think of this part.' Then a discussion may follow in which suggestions are shared.

LESSON FORM

The following is a suggested format for a lesson which, whilst having some degree of form, at the same time allows freedom for exploration.

Main movement idea

Before a lesson can be planned, the teacher must decide what the main movement idea will be, for this guides the whole lesson.

Choice of movement ideas comes from the movement content, as outlined in Part I, and emphasises either activities, dynamics, space, or relationships. Examples are given in the lessons in Part III.

Rhythmical introduction

The introduction, being the first movement experience of the lesson, must be very rhythmical as this immediately catches the children's interest. It should be chosen where possible to match or to contrast with the mood of the class and so lead them smoothly into the lesson. The teacher should always direct this initial experience.

Movement experiences

There now follows a series of experiences which are designed to teach the children something about the main movement idea. Examples of these are given in *How does a movement idea grow?* in Part III.

There should be three or four of these short activities in each lesson and they should afford the children contrasting situations. If they have been vigorously jumping, a more gentle experience should come next. Specific teaching and freedom for exploration are both possible here.

Dance form

This is a blending of the movement experiences to produce a dance which has a clear beginning and then develops towards a satisfying end. The children should be able to repeat the whole dance at least three times in any lesson. Alternatively, the teacher or the children may decide initially what the dance will be about and can then choose a main movement idea and appropriate experiences to bring about this dance. An example of this is seen in the *Sea Storm* dance in Part III.

The amount of time spent on each part of the lesson will vary according to the needs of the class. On the introduction of a new movement idea more time may be spent on the movement experiences than on the dance form. As the children gain more understanding, the time spent on the creative work on the dance will be much more than that spent on the earlier part of the lesson. The average length of the complete lesson will also vary. Initially it may be short but can be extended as the children become more experienced and so have a greater contribution to make.

At the end of a lesson or series of lessons the teacher will wish to assess the improvement and progress in the children's ability and understanding. This may be evaluated according to the three main areas of development suggested in Part IV:

(a) Has there been an increase in physical skill?
   e.g. Are the children jumping higher than before?

(b) Have the children experienced something new?
   e.g. Have they worked in a group for the first time?

(c) Are the children responding more quickly when the lesson allows for a creative situation? Have they more ideas to offer?

If the answers are positive then the children should be having a worthwhile and satisfying lesson.

PART III

What do we dance about ?

Movement ideas

Since it is with movement that we are concerned, our main source of ideas lies in the natural movement of children. A dance experience or expressive movement lesson can grow from a very simple movement idea.

One example of a movement idea might be to move through different levels in space—high and low—interpreted as the *up and down of movement* or *rising and sinking* or *'enjoying gravity'*. The children thereby experience something of what it means to move from high to low and from low to high and so they become aware of changing sensations and of the possibilities of expression.

Each of the many movement ideas will give the children a new and different experience, the summation of which, for each child, is a rich store of knowledge and understanding of expressive movement, to be called upon as he requires it in the creative situation.

How does a movement idea grow?

Once the movement idea has been chosen, the next step is to find challenging and exciting ways of presenting the idea to the children as movement experiences. A great variety of movement experiences are to be found within the idea of the *up and down of movement.* If this does not go beyond stretching to reach up then coming down again, it can be dull and uninteresting and will not capture the child in the excitement of rhythmical movement. What will make it fun? The possibilities are many:

(*a*) 'Reach up (or rise) quickly and sink very slowly. Let's try it the other way.'

This has been made more challenging by emphasising the dynamics within the idea, i.e. by the change of speed.

(*b*) 'Shoot up until you are pulled off the floor altogether, then come down fast, ready to shoot up again.'

This expansion on the original idea appears simple but it is through emphasis on dynamics, i.e. change of speed, and on relationship with the floor, that the activity of jumping is introduced.

(c) 'Can you go just a little way up the first time, and come back; a little farther up the next time, and then the whole way the next time?'

The emphasis here is on extension into space which sets up 'graduated' movement. This has very clear rhythmical phrasing with the climax at the topmost point in the movement.

(d) 'It can be funny if you rise up with part of your body at a time, one arm, one foot, your back and now your head, and collapse all at once on the floor.'

By placing emphasis on parts of the body, the original up-and-down movement has become much more interesting.

(e) 'Perhaps as you go up this time, you could turn all the way to the top. Are you going to turn on the way down or come straight down?'

A new activity, turning, has been introduced here.

(f) 'Can you help each other to go up and down?'
'Can you look as if you are really pulling your "heavy" partner up, or can you show that you can lower him very slowly and quietly to the floor?'
'Can you make a dance about helping someone to enjoy going up and down; someone who has always been very near the floor and does not know what it is like higher up?'

Relationship with a partner is important in this exploration of the *up and down of movement.*

These examples of the development of the *up and down of movement* show how a simple idea can be made more interesting and more challenging for the children. Each experience makes particular demands on them but the teacher should expect a good degree of understanding and a high standard of performance.

29

3 Rising and sinking in a group

In the following three lessons it is suggested how some of these more interesting explorations into change of level can be incorporated into a dance. Guidance is given for the teaching which precedes the dance form of the lesson. In the dance the children see how the independent explorations contribute towards a formed and creative experience.

Lessons arising out of the *up and down of movement*

LESSON A
Main movement idea

the *up and down of movement*, incorporating turning and jumping, changes in speed, and also stillness

Rhythmical introduction

The children look at their hands and then place them on the floor. The teacher moves a tambour up and down, away from and back to the floor, and the children follow this movement with their hands. Stillness may be achieved by a question such as: 'Can you stop at the same place as the tambour when it stops?'

Teaching: (i) the tambour is not played but acts as a visual stimulus.

(ii) the movement of the tambour should be rhythmically phrased:
up . . . down . . . up . . . down-up-still
down-up . . . down-up . . . down-still.

(iii) a lively following of the tambour at different levels results in movement of the whole body up and down, and a spirited and responsive atmosphere can be built up in the room.

(iv) through this game-like introduction the children become aware of the extremes of up and down, and also of stages in between when the tambour is stopped unexpectedly.

30

Movement experiences

1 The children now follow their hands up and down instead of following the tambour. They choose their own speed and rhythm.

Teaching: The children should stop often and be still, and then move on again. There are two reasons for this:

(*a*) it encourages rhythmic phrasing;

(*b*) it makes the children aware of *where* they stop—high, low or in between.

2 The children still follow their hands but now they increase the strength and speed of their movement so that they shoot up from the floor so strongly and quickly that they begin jumping. These jumps may take them to another place in the room.

Teaching: (i) some of the more lively children may already be jumping as a result of experience 1. If so, a demonstration by these children could introduce the idea. (ii) challenge the children to shoot through space—long, thin and fully stretched, feet and legs pushing strongly against the floor and hands and head shooting far away from the floor.

3 It is now necessary to phrase the jumping so that it can be appreciated as a rhythmical experience. This may be achieved:
(i) by asking the children to shoot into the air three times only and then to be still on the spot before setting off to jump again;
(ii) by the teacher playing a rhythmical phrase on the tambour to give the class a common rhythm.

Teaching: (i) in (i) above, the children dictate their own rhythm and tempo and so may be more successful at jumping, whereas in (ii), although the standard of jumping may be less good since the tempo will not suit all the children, they have a very clear, rhythmical experience.
(ii) the children need help to improve their physical skill in jumping: (*a*) in pushing off strongly, using the feet and legs to leave the floor; (*b*) in bending and releasing just enough tension in the legs to be able to meet the floor and yet be ready to shoot off again.

31

4 The activity now changes from jumping to turning. The children begin low near the floor and rise up, turning as they go. When they reach as high as they can go, they may be asked: 'How are you going to come down— turning or straight?'

Teaching: The children should be given time to explore this new idea and to decide how they want to do it.

5 All the children now perform the turning up and down in time to a common rhythm played by the teacher on the cymbal.

Teaching: (i) the cymbal is used here as it has more resonance and so can give the feeling of continuous movement, going up and down and round.
(ii) the tempo may be changed. When the cymbal is played faster the turns also become faster, slowing down again as the cymbal is played more slowly. (The technique of playing the cymbal is explained in Part V.)

Dance form

The movement experiences are now formed into a short dance which should be repeated two or three times.

From a still position near the floor the children begin by turning slowly as they rise. They then sink, still turning or else going straight down. This may be repeated about three times, each time getting a little faster. On the third rising, the turning breaks into jumping and this takes the children to another place in the room. The jumping phrase may also be repeated. The children finish the dance by sinking down slowly —following their hands—to finish in stillness near the floor.

Teaching: To guide the order of events, the teacher should accompany on the cymbal the turning and the final sinking. The jumping may be unaccompanied but, if an accompaniment is needed, the tambour would be the appropriate instrument.

LESSON B

This lesson is a development of lesson A in that it originates from the same movement idea and shares some of the

experiences, but it puts particular emphasis on:
changes in strength: strong, light, heavy
changes in speed: quick, slow.

Rhythmical introduction

As for lesson A

Teaching: The tambour may be moved up and down with unexpected changes in speed to give the children the sensation of swiftness.

Movement experiences

1 The children continue to follow the tambour as it rises and falls and stops. Introduce into the stillness the sensation of gripping firmly on to the floor with the feet, and the feeling of strength in the legs. This makes the children aware of the strength of the stillness which dissolves as they move on again to follow the tambour.

Teaching: (i) the tambour moves in silence but one or two strong, rapid beats, when the children become still, complement the feeling of strength. This sound can act as an extra signal for stillness, to support the visual one.
(ii) help the children to appreciate the strength of the stillness with such instructions as: 'Grip with your legs'; 'Press firmly into the floor'; 'Draw your elbows near to your body'.
The use of the words 'grip' and 'press' should encourage muscular activity which will have the accompanying sensation of strength.

2 The pausing, as a contrast, is light and high with just enough tension in the body to make it feel as if the body were resting on air—almost as if it were holding its breath before moving on!

Teaching: (i) the children may no longer need the visual stimulus of the tambour.
(ii) the signal for pausing may be given by Indian bells which are helpful in setting the atmosphere.
(iii) it may help to suggest to the boys in particular that a great deal of skill is required to balance so lightly in stillness.

3 In contrast to this light, balancing stillness, the children
may collapse heavily on to the floor. The whole body may
collapse at once or only part of the body at a time. The
phrasing should be: rising to hold lightly in stillness, then
collapsing into heavy stillness, rising again, and repeat.

Teaching: (i) the use of the word 'rising' as opposed to 'rise'
suggests to the children that this action is prolonged in time
and is not produced quickly. This lets them appreciate fully
the contrast between lightness in rising and heaviness in the
more sudden collapse.
(ii) the contrast should help the children to experience and
understand different sensations in stillness.
(iii) the period of stillness may be governed by the children's
timing or it may be stimulated and timed by a sound or words
from the teacher.

4 Repeat part 4 of lesson A. This time the emphasis is on
turning upwards slowly and lightly, and turning downwards
with 'fast or slow strength', as if boring into the ground.

Teaching: (i) the use of words to create atmosphere for the
children is an extremely important part of the presentation
of an expressive movement lesson. The phrase 'fast or slow
strength' should suggest a purposeful sinking movement.
(ii) if the children choose to come down strongly and quickly
they may have difficulty with balance. Suggest that they
attempt at the end of the turn either to hold the body still
or to allow it to become heavy and collapse.

Dance form

This may be a repeat of lesson A, but the emphasis this time
should be on the changing strengths and speeds. For example,
the children might finish the third repetition of the dance
with a heavy collapse on to the floor, since this is a sensation
which children enjoy. Alternatively, if they indicate that they
have ideas of their own, they may enjoy making their own
dance about the *up and down of movement*, drawing on
the experiences of the two lessons.

In order to give them a finish to the dance which is satisfying
in terms of rhythm and quality, the children might be asked
to bring their own dance to a low situation, near the floor,

when they hear the cymbal beginning to play. This prepares
them for joining with the teacher in a final unison dance
with accompaniment. It may be that the cymbal leads them
in a fast rising turn which stops strongly, followed by a
slower, drifting turn back to the floor. On the second repetition
of this, the slow return could be even slower, and so until the last
time when it becomes very slow indeed, the children controlling
the lowering to the floor with, perhaps, a heavy collapse
at the last moment.

LESSON C

This a further lesson on the idea of changing levels or the
up and down of movement. Relationship is developed now.
The children work with a partner and create a more dramatic
situation.

Rhythmical introduction

Instead of following the movement of the tambour in the
teacher's hands, the children work in pairs now, and one
child's hands try to follow his partner's hands which are
moving up and down.

Teaching: If the children can co-operate well this becomes
a game-like situation with one child trying to lose the 'follower'.
Alternatively, they might aim to stop together when the
teacher gives a signal on the tambour.

Movement experiences

1 One partner becomes the stronger of the two and without
actually touching he uses his strength to press his partner
down towards the floor, perhaps straight down or perhaps
turning. Initially his partner is submissive but then he reacts.
This reaction may take many forms and the children can
explore the possibilities.

Teaching: (i) the resolving of this movement phrase may
be left entirely to the children, or it may be guided by the
teacher who selects possible reactions to the strong downward pressure. In either case, the following might be seen:
(*a*) the balance of power may change and the situation slowly
be reversed; (*b*) the submissive partner may roll out of the

way very suddenly, recover quickly and take on the role of the strong partner; (c) the reaction of the weaker of the two may be so strong and sudden that it throws both partners into a jump.
(ii) if the children's ideas are slow to come, the teacher should let them experience each of these reactions in turn.

Dance form

The dance could begin with the game-like experience of chasing a partner's hands, as in the rhythmical introduction. This becomes more 'serious' until it develops into the stronger and the weaker—height indicating strength, lowness indicating weakness. There is a constant exchange of roles incorporating strong pressure followed by appropriate reactions. The final situation is worked out by each couple and their stillness at the end should show clearly how the dance has finished.

Further movement ideas for lessons

As the movement ideas for lessons arise out of the observation of children, it is natural that some ideas will stress activities, some dynamics, some space and some relationships.
The following ideas for lessons in these four areas can be developed in a way similar to that suggested for the *up and down of movement* which emphasises space.

Activities

Stepping and travelling: the contrast between the 'contained' sensation of each step and the feeling of going through space.
Jumping and turning: the very different appeal of (a) the freedom of leaping and leaving the ground, and (b) the seeming endlessness of going round and round.

Dynamics

Growing and diminishing strength: the gentle quality of diminishing strength as opposed to the powerful and sometimes explosive quality of increasing strength; the difference in sensation of moving really fast for a long time or for just a moment, or the calming effect which moving slowly and

36

carefully has upon such urgency of movement. The rhythmical possibilities of these actions are clear.

Space

Expanding and drawing in: the contrast between spreading the whole body outwards and pulling everything back towards the centre of the body, thus giving the differing sensations of being open and of being closed in.
Moving in and out of different levels: being aware of the pull of gravity and its effect on movement.
Drawing patterns on the floor: the awareness of such activities as travelling or stepping, and making special shapes or patterns on the floor:
'Can your curved patterns get smaller and smaller till they stop altogether?'
'Can you move in curves around your partner's very straight pathways?'

Relationships

Moving towards/away from/around: either a spot on the floor or some object, a partner or a group, may be chosen, but this will enable the children to perceive the relationship between themselves and something or someone. This is a necessary experience if movement is to be at all expressive.
Parts of the body in relation to each other: several possibilities for movement in one foot chasing the other foot or one hand meeting, moving with and parting from the other hand.

There are countless other such ideas waiting to be found in the movement of children. They can find many for themselves. There follow three lessons which develop three of these ideas and which stress activities, dynamics and relationships respectively. (The lessons on the *up and down of movement* have already concentrated on space.)

No lesson can be formed on one aspect alone, so it will be seen that each lesson has subsidiary ideas from other areas supporting its main movement idea.

LESSON

This lesson emphasises activities since the main movement idea is that of *jumping and turning*, incorporating contrasts in speed and level.

Rhythmical introduction

rhythmical jumping to tambour accompaniment:
    jump and jump and jump and jump
    and jump and jump and still!

Movement experiences

1 The first experience is jumping, in which the height of the jumps is very important—jumping 'to fly high into the air'.

    Teaching: (i) the exuberant freedom of the jumping and leaping of young children should be appreciated here.
    (ii) rhythmical phrasing may be encouraged by asking the children to settle low near the floor after one or two jumps.

2 The children are now asked to turn instead of jumping. The link with 1 may be made as follows: 'Now you have jumped on to a spot on the floor. Can you turn round and round on that spot, gently and slowly?'

    Teaching: The teacher should control the number of turns since the children can very quickly become giddy.

3 'Can you turn round very fast? Stop now, and go the other way this time!'

    Teaching: (i) again, to prevent giddiness, the children should turn for only brief spells.
    (ii) 2 and 3 will let the children experience both slow and quick turning and the different sensations of each. Some children may be happier doing one rather than the other.

4 'Your feet have been taking you round and round on the floor; now sit down and spin round as you sit—spin and stop and spin and stop.'

    Teaching: (i) children usually enjoy this method of turning. They like to try to get a strong push off from their hands

38

4 Jumping 'to fly high into the air'

and then put feet and hands on the floor quickly to stop the spin.

(ii) an accompaniment on the cymbal (see p. 84) can help to phrase this and make the sudden stop exciting.

5   As a contrast to turning low near the floor the children should now try to turn very high away from the floor.

Teaching: (i) the children appreciate the sensation of height if they are on tiptoe with hands stretching high above them.

(ii) accompaniment on Indian bells augments the feeling of height.

6   The children can now have fun listening to the accompaniment: when they hear the cymbal they spin on their hips, when they hear the Indian bells they change to turning, high up.

Teaching: Short spells of each activity give the children contrasting experiences and a rhythmical change.

Dance form

The children begin by spinning on the floor. When they hear the Indian bells they begin turning higher and higher. When the bells stop they jump and jump and jump to another place in the room, turning high in this new place until the cymbal plays, when they spin on the floor until it stops.

Teaching: This is a lively dance which can be repeated as often as wished. It will require constant recharging, by the playing of the instruments or by the teacher's voice, to lead the children into each change of idea and movement.

LESSON

This lesson emphasises dynamics since the main movement idea is that of *a contrast of strong and light qualities,* incorporating increase in speed and awareness of different areas of the floor.

Rhythmical introduction

The teacher plays a rhythm on the tambour or claps out a

40

rhythm and the class repeat it by clapping or by beating on the floor with their hands. This is repeated many times until the rhythm is established. The teacher and class then play the rhythm together, letting it get faster and faster.

Teaching: A suitable rhythm might be: short, short, long—short, short, long—short, short, long, long, long.

Movement experiences

1 The feet now take over the rhythm, beginning slowly and strongly then becoming faster and faster.

   Teaching: (i) the children should feel the strength of their feet and legs against the floor.
   (ii) the teacher may need to control the speeding up by means of a rhythmical accompaniment on the tambour.

2 The next activity is a development of the first. As the feet speed up the rhythm, becoming very fast, so they want to jump strongly off the floor.

   Teaching: (i) the rhythmic accompaniment from the tambour begins slowly, accelerates, then slows down again.
   (ii) a rhythmic phrase can thus be built up: beating time with the feet→accelerating→jumping→repeat.

3 The mood changes now. After this very vigorous rhythmical experience the children are asked to sink low to the floor. From there the children follow their hands as they lead them up, turning all the time, till they are up high, and then the hands lead them down again to the floor. This turning should be gentle and slow.

   Teaching: (i) the phrasing of the turn can be greatly assisted if the children think of breathing in as they rise and turn and breathing out very quietly as they sink and turn.
   (ii) the feet were the focus of attention previously; now attention switches to the hands.

4 The turning becomes stronger now—short, sharp, strong turns, then a very quick halt: turn, hold . . . turn, hold.

   Teaching: (i) the strength of this movement should be stressed.

(ii) if the children find difficulty in balancing, they should concentrate on stopping low down, with their feet spread well apart.

(iii) when using the cymbal as accompaniment, the instrument can be caught between the fingers to stop the sound. This helps the children to hold position.

Dance form

The dance begins at a place on the floor where there is a strong and powerful influence. The children move away from this spot to another where the influence is much lighter, but this too gradually becomes strong.

The children begin by beating the rhythm on the floor with their hands; on a signal from the teacher they start beating with the feet instead and this accelerates into vigorous jumping upon the spot on the floor. When the cymbal plays the children begin turning and stopping. This turning pulls them away from their original place and they eventually stop at a new spot on the floor. Here the atmosphere is quite different and the children can turn lightly, but soon they are drawn back down and the whole dance begins again from this new spot.

LESSON

Music accompanies this lesson. It is selected from *Listen, Move and Dance* records which are listed on page 86. Two pieces which show a contrast in dynamics have been chosen:

A, from *Listen, Move and Dance* 1. Side 1. Band 3.

B, from *Listen, Move and Dance* 2. Side 2. Band 4.

The dance is in two parts, both of which are concerned with relationships since the main movement idea is that of *the relationship of one hand to the other,* incorporating various activities and dynamic changes as stimulated by the music chosen.

Rhythmical introduction

The children hear music A and immediately let their hands dance about in time to the music. Sometimes the two hands will be far away from each other, sometimes they will come

43

5   A vigorous jump

so close together that they can clap in time to the music.

Teaching: (i) this allows the children to listen to the music and become familiar with it as soon as possible.
(ii) if the children sit on the floor, they will find it easier to concentrate on moving their hands.

Movement experiences

1 While sitting on the floor, the children allow one hand to escape but they very quickly snatch it back with the other hand.

Teaching: (i) the slow movement of the first hand should contrast with the sudden movement of the second hand.
(ii) the children should be encouraged to send away the first hand in all directions.

2 The first hand now extends further and perhaps makes the body roll over or stretch fully or even move to another place on the floor before being snatched back.

Teaching: (i) these explorations are unaccompanied since all the exploration rhythms are different at this point.
(ii) the children should aim to get the first hand as far away as possible.

3 The children are now on their feet and the hand escapes so far this time that they have to jump right into the air to get it back.

Teaching: (i) the whole body should be fully stretched as the second hand reaches after the first.
(ii) the music is introduced again here and the children encouraged to follow it, if possible.

4 The escaping hand leads the body into a wide and open turn, then the other hand, catching up, closes the body again and brings the turn to a stop.

Teaching: This should be tried immediately with the music.

Dance form

A The music is played and this time the children compose their own 'hand-chasing' dance using the above actions

44

and introducing any new ideas of their own. The music
will give the dance form and rhythm.
This part of the dance must finish with one hand on the
floor and the other hand holding it prisoner. The children
may need to practise this.

B The second half of the dance using music B may be taught
immediately after dancing part A.
The trapped hand pushes strongly against the other, trying
to get away from the floor. Each time it has a little success
but then collapses, to be trapped again. This happens as often
as the children wish until, at the end of the music, the hand is
finally successful and bursts free.
The children may then decide whether to finish the dance
there or to repeat part A.

It would be advisable to have the music on tape as one
piece needs to flow on from the other.

The following lessons make particular use of percussion. Each
may be taught separately or one may be a development of
another.

LESSON A

Main movement ideas

accented metrical rhythms;
children's own rhythms;
stepping; turning; jumping.

The teacher plays percussion to stimulate and accompany
the movement.

Rhythmical introduction

The children are asked to clap their hands together freely
until a signal from the teacher's drum indicates stillness. This
can be repeated several times. The teacher then plays a simple
2/4 or 4/4 rhythm on the drum and the children play it back
by clapping. Teacher and children play it together.
Alternatively, the teacher may reverse the order of these
activities, starting the lesson with unison response to the drum
rhythm, followed by the children's own rhythms.

Movement experiences

1 The rhythmic possibilities of the introduction may also
apply to the feet.

Teaching: (i) the children should be encouraged to make
their own rhythms uneven and free in contrast to the
teacher's measured rhythm.
(ii) they should listen carefully to the drum rhythm and
make their feet keep time to it.
(iii) they should be encouraged to use their feet in stepping,
in jumping with both feet together or on one foot (hopping),
and in tapping both loudly and softly against the floor
with heels, toes and the edges of the feet.

2 The same rhythmic ideas can now be employed by the
hands beating or tapping against the floor, and against
other parts of the body such as back, thighs or hips.

Teaching: (i) beating alternately against the floor and
high above the head as if against the air can be a very
active movement for a lively class and affords them an
example of accent in sound and silence. It may be necessary
to slow down the tempo since the children's hands will
require more time to move up and down.
(ii) the children can be made aware of tension contrasts,
e.g. a powerful beat against the floor for loud sounds, a
more gentle tap against parts of the body for softer ones.

Dance form

The experiences in the introduction and in 1 and 2 can now
be put together and repeated several times to form the dance.
For example, the children's own clapping rhythm : drum signal :
the teacher's rhythm in unison : the children's own foot
rhythm : drum signal : the teacher's rhythm in unison : the
children's own body percussion rhythm : drum signal : the
teacher's rhythm in unison.

3 The teacher plays the Indian bells and the children listen
without moving for the length of time the sound lasts.
As soon as the music begins again, the children start to
turn gently and they go on moving until it stops. Next time,
they creep until the music stops. Lastly, they may choose
either turning or creeping.

The bells are then struck together in a rhythm identical to that in 1 and 2. The children respond as they please or beat out the rhythm with hands and feet simultaneously.

LESSON B

This is a development of Lesson A.

Main movement ideas

measured rhythms;
changes of strength and/or speed;
possible relationship with a partner.

Percussion is played by the children themselves.

Rhythmical introduction

The children march or jump in time to a measured rhythm played on a drum by the teacher.

Teaching: This may be a repeat of the rhythm used in the previous lesson.

Movement experiences

1 *Either*: the teacher may decide to distribute the tambourines, drums and 'coffee-tins' at this early point. It is desirable that there should be sufficient instruments for one between two. The children take turns at playing the same rhythm as in the introduction, or one of their own, while the other child dances.

   Or: the teacher recalls the whole of the drum section of the previous dance, repeating it several times. This demands a good standard of achievement. She then distributes the drums, etc., one between two, and the rhythm is repeated, one child playing for the other to dance.

2 This part of the lesson demands more creativity from the children. The partners are asked to experiment, making sounds on the drum and coupling this with suitable move-ment, e.g.

   (*a*) a fluttering of the finger-tips and finger nails against the skin, wood or metal of the drum suggests delicate and lively movements of the head, hands or feet as they travel over the floor;

(*b*) a continuous scraping of the finger nails against the skin suggests turning;

(*c*) a staccato beating of the palm of the hand against the skin suggests vigorous jumping;

(*d*) dropping the hand heavily against the skin suggests low, lurching steps giving in to the pull of gravity.

Teaching: (i) the teacher may give help indirectly, moving about the class offering advice to individual couples. For example, varying the height of the hand during the staccato beating can stimulate the dancer to vary the power of the jumps, especially if he watches the drumming partner's hand.
(ii) the teacher may wish the whole class to act in unison; this she controls and teaches, and she may accompany the class herself. The children could be asked, for example, to make single limbs, as opposed to the whole body, slump downwards without tension.

Dance form

The partners are asked to make their own dance, selecting from the percussion sounds with which they have experimented. Each child creates his own solo, being helped and accompanied by his partner.
The children may need advice on how to finish the dance. For example, the percussion partner may play faster and faster, culminating in a sudden loud sound; or the opposite, getting slower and softer as the dancer's movements die down into stillness. Another possibility is that, at a suitable moment, the teacher breaks in with her own percussion-play to bring the dance to a close.

LESSON C

This is not one lesson but a concentration of ideas which can result from the initial dance experiences with percussion, and which are designed to contribute to group work. Prerequisites are (*a*) availability of a range of percussion instruments and

48

(*b*) for the children, either some dance experience with percussion or familiarity with the method of working with their teacher in an experimental or exploratory situation.

The teacher can select from the following to form the lesson:

Main movement ideas
use of percussion in groups, linking a particular action to a particular instrument;
rhythms which arise from repeated actions.

These help towards initiating group sensitivity.

Rhythmical introduction
Let the children bounce on their feet without leaving the floor, the heels making a rhythmic sound against the floor. This should be contrasted with several jumps of even height.

Next should be phrases of heel beating and controlled jumping in unison, accompanied by a small drum. The change of tempo required for the two contrasting phrases should be noted.

Movement experiences
The children need to widen their repertoire of movement activities so that they may make a selection for group work. This may be achieved in various ways; two are outlined here:

A *Teacher-controlled*:

1 The drum is played at various speeds and strengths to stimulate different kinds of jumps of varying heights.

  Teaching: (i) taking off from, and landing on, one foot, or from two feet and back to one, should be encouraged. (ii) the children should try high jumps or interesting movements of the legs while in the air.

2 The cymbal is played for turning, building up the sound for turns of increasing speed. The cymbal should be struck then swung about in the air to stimulate undulating, travelling turns. A sudden quenching of the sound suggests quick, sharp turns.

Teaching: Let the children try turning at very high and very low levels, and also turns which are started by the legs or the arms being swung out and around the body.

3 Shakers or maraccas may be played rhythmically to stimulate step patterns, or played in quick phrases of sound for travelling with hurried steps.

Teaching: (i) let the children walk on unusual parts of the feet or with brushing gestures of the instep or toes. (ii) they may enjoy stepping rhythmically on unusual parts of the body, e.g. from one hip to the other in a sitting position, or on hands and feet simultaneously.

4 Ascending or descending notes may be played on the cymbal or piano for rising and sinking movements, being gestures of the whole body towards and away from the floor.

Teaching: Good quality of movement should be stressed. The children should attempt such expressions as smoothness with speed or contrasting quick, jerky movements.

B *Children experimenting and observing*:

The children are asked to try out different ways of jumping. The teacher then chooses several good examples to stimulate variety. Next, the children are asked to create little repeatable jumping phrases, as in the rhythmical introduction. The teacher is observing and chooses two or three of the children's phrases which she accompanies on a drum. The class observes and finally selects one which all the children do, accompanied by the teacher or perhaps by the child whose idea it was. They may then return to their own phrase, improving upon it in the light of the shared experience.

A similar process is used for turning, stepping, travelling, rising and sinking.
Another idea is to use a combination of methods A and B, e.g. jumping as explored in B, and turning as in A.

Dance form

Let the children choose the activity which interests them and form groups accordingly; a group should not be larger

6 Jumping with interesting shapes

than six or seven people. It may be necessary to duplicate some popular activity. Choosing their own instrumentalists, the groups now form their own short dance, basing it on their chosen activity and referring to the ideas which emerged during the exploratory part of the lesson.

Here is an example of the kind of group dance the teacher may hope to see emerging:

A jumping group begins by bouncing close together, as in the rhythmical introduction, then the drum played by one child stimulates the group into making little jumps on the spot. With each jump, the group as a whole may turn to face different directions. The drummer takes an energetic leap, accompanied by a loud sound, and arrives in another part of the room. By playing his drum he then entices the rest of the group to join him, which they do either individually or as a whole group, using rhythmical jumping phrases which allow them to travel. They finish close together, the jumping dying down into stillness.

From such beginnings, group dance 'happenings' can grow, allowing the teacher and/or class members to practise the art of choreography. Group dances so formed, using percussion accompaniment, are particularly useful for including contributions from children who are temporarily or permanently prevented from fully active participation in movement lessons. They can act as instrumentalists and can help the teacher with observation. They may advise small groups or help to plan the final class dance.

Imaginative themes

So far, the stimulus for lessons has come from the children's movement. This is not the only starting point. An idea for an expressive movement lesson may come from a source which is familiar to the children but which they are not likely to have appreciated in terms of movement.
We begin by appealing to the children's imagination which yields a dance idea centred round, for example, a battle scene from history. Since the initial starting point has not been movement itself, the first step towards developing this idea is to

52

translate it into rhythmical phrases of movement. This necessitates careful planning on the part of the teacher to ensure that the children are immediately appreciating the theme through moving, which is quite different from looking, or reading, or talking.

Selecting a theme from such a source usually means that the dance form is already clearly established. Events as they appear establish the form, whereas when movement itself is the source the final dance form is freer and perhaps more creative.

If the chosen theme is a battle scene, it can be translated in many ways. It is full of movement possibilities and the class and teacher can decide upon which aspect of the battle they will concentrate, and how it will be conducted and resolved.

Appropriate questions are:

'Are you going to "fight" this battle one against one so that you highlight individual combat?'

'Do you want to show the strength of the armies on the march and the eventual disintegration of the conquered and the triumph of the victors?'

'Are you going to show the rhythm of battle in the forwards and backwards of conflict?'

Depending on the era of the battle, knowledge of the weapons used and the fighting methods could provide interesting movement possibilities for older children.

If the children want to have the assembling of two armies in their dance at some point, how can this be depicted? The answer lies in such questions as:

What activities? stepping, marching, and other drill manoeuvres.

What dynamics? strong, deliberate, rhythmical pattern.

What shape of marching pattern? forward, —2 —3 —4, side, side (with a turn of the head).

What grouping? blocks of four with change of leaders.

Much of this planning can be done by the children themselves but guidance at various stages and with different groups may vary.

'What happens when one army meets the enemy?' 'How can you show the to-and-fro of battle?' 'Do you each have individual combat with one of the enemy?'

This could result in small forward/backward or up/down conflicts where no physical contact is made but the direction of the movement indicates the relative strengths. The victorious army could then re-form and leave the defeated motionless on the field, and could repeat the initial marching pattern in order to move on. Alternatively, the defeated could retreat with a new rhythmical pattern suggesting heaviness, while the victors stand still in triumph.

Whatever form this battle takes, there should be an early attempt to build clear, rhythmical movement patterns which can be repeated within the dance, and to ensure that the whole battle can eventually be repeated almost exactly because the form and content are so clear. This satisfies the children since they know that they have a finished piece of work which they can now share with others. They have also had an opportunity to be involved in a situation of conflict and resolution in a way which may be different from their previous experience.

The situation must be avoided where all the children simply line up and 'shoot' each other. This would not be translating the idea into the medium of expressive movement but would be encroaching on the realm of mime. The children must be given a complete movement experience which is physically challenging and rhythmically satisfying.

The children have a great deal to gain from discussion throughout the period of work on the development of an idea. Therefore, if they have been working in small groups, they should be encouraged to speak about the problems of bringing their idea to final form and about the experience as it was for them.

7a The vanquished . . .

7c the victor

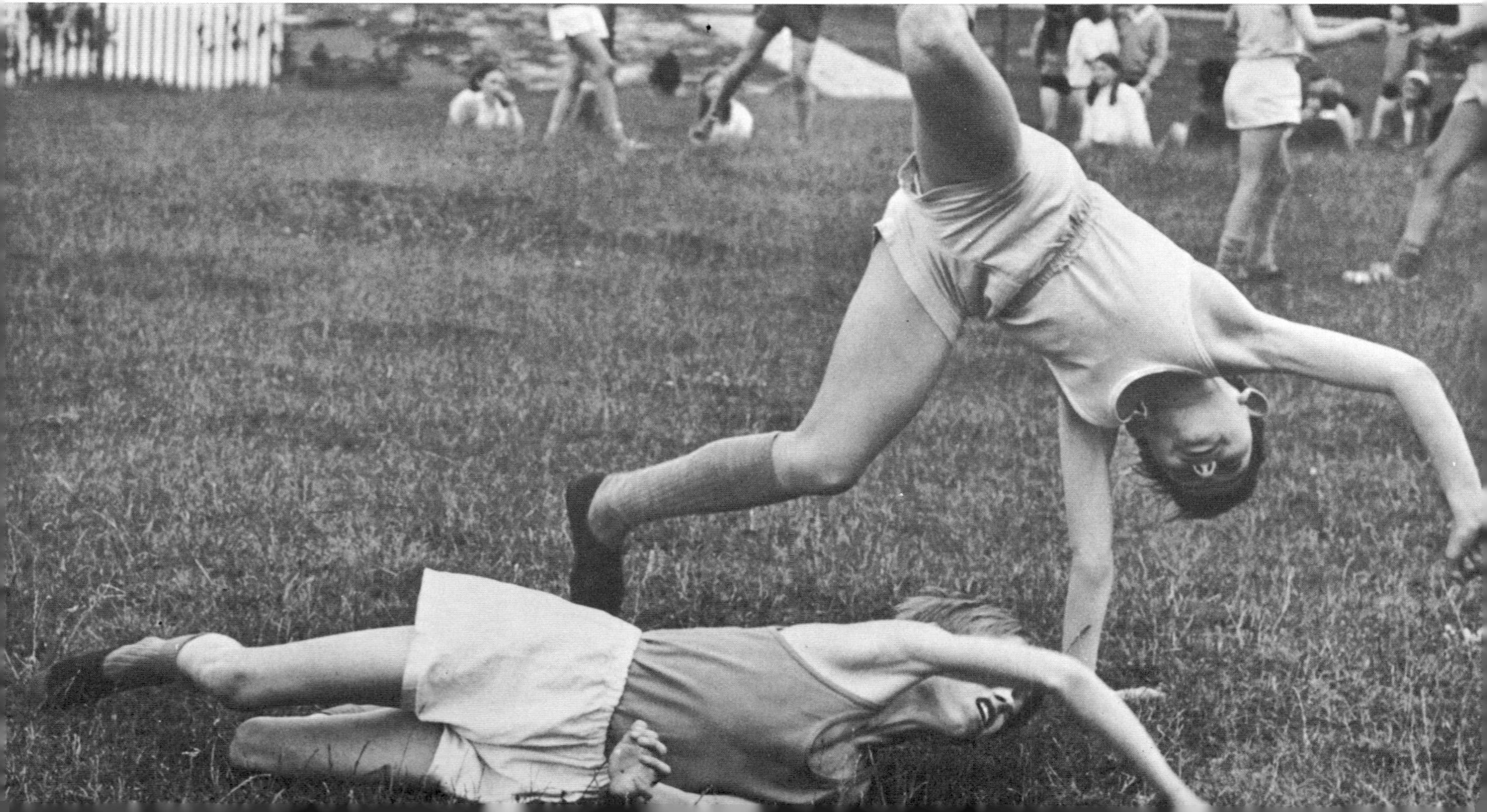

The following three lessons are based on imaginative themes:

LESSON

Magic Boots

Accompaniment: any lively tune from one of the records listed on page 86.

Main movement ideas

turning; jumping; hopping;
skipping; galloping; stepping.

The children are each wearing a pair of magic boots. These boots dance about just as they like when the music plays and do not stop until the music stops. It is only when there is no music that the boots will do as they are asked. This gives an opportunity for spontaneous movement contrasted with controlled activities which the children all try together.

Rhythmical introduction

The boots set off when the music plays. In contrast, there are short spells of silence, when the children have a rest, before the boots begin to dance again with the music.

Teaching: Young children enjoy the free response to the music at this stage.

Movement experiences

in the silence:

1 'Can you make your boots jump high in the air?'
   'Make them both go very far from the floor!'

2 'Try to keep your boots together and touching each other all the time.'

3 'Maybe your boots could take very big steps this time.'
   'How far can you make each boot go?'

4 'How small can you make your steps?'
   'You are hardly moving at all, going very slowly.'

5 'How fast can you make the boots go all over the floor?'

All these actions are contrasted with the playing of the music and the boots going off on their own—turning and jumping and perhaps going over the children's heads as they turn upside down. The boots may enjoy turning since this is not included in 1 to 5.

Note: It is important that in the experiences 1 to 5 the children concentrate on making the boots do as they are told and do it well.

Dance form

The boots are put on.
The music plays, and stops.
What can the boots be made to do?

The music interrupts this, then stops again; and so on, till the children rush to pull the boots off and collapse exhausted on the floor.

Teaching: (i) the length of the musical periods should be irregular so that there is an element of surprise for the children. (ii) the teacher should indicate which of the actions, 1 to 5, will come next so that the children are clear about what to do.

LESSON

The Sea Storm

When the inspiration for a lesson or a dance is an imaginative theme such as a sea storm, some care must be taken to ensure that the main movement idea and the ensuing movement experiences are appropriate to such a theme. In order to do this, the following questions must be asked:

What *activities* would be appropriate?
What *dynamic aspects* are recognisable in a stormy sea?
What *spatial changes* might take place?
Would some *relationships or groups* convey the theme better than others?

The whirling, rushing and tossing of the water can be shown by turning, travelling and jumping with increasing and decreasing speed and strength. Spatially, a calm sea will be on a medium level but a rising and sinking which increases in size will indicate the storm. Relationship may at first be that of individuals

mingling amongst each other to indicate the stirring water, while later, a group rhythm of tossing may depict the rising intensity of the storm.

The lesson can be built up from this.

Rhythmical introduction

short bursts of quick travel, followed by a pause

Teaching: (i) this activity could be accompanied by shaking the tambourine then pausing. This gives the class a common rhythm.

(ii) slight change of level throughout the movement should be encouraged here so that the children pause at a higher level than they move.

Movement experiences

1 Similar to the introduction, but the third 'rushing' phrase should lead into tossing the whole body into the air two or three times:

> rush . . . pause; rush . . . pause;
> rush . . . toss, toss, toss . . . sink.

Teaching: (i) the children need time to practise the rushing into tossing. The change from *forward* rushing into *upward* tossing may mean that the children have to slow down slightly just before the tossing.

(ii) the children could try to 'throw off' the ends of their body—i.e. hands, feet, head—as they toss the whole body into the air, and could try to 'collect' them again as they come down.

(iii) as the tossing is rhythmically different for each child, the accompaniment might now be the children's voices only, e.g. 'Wooo-oosh!'.

2 In between one phrase of *rush . . . pause* and the next can now be inserted a backward sucking movement so that the phrase becomes: rush . . . pause; pull back; rush . . . (high) pause; pull back; rush . . . toss, toss, toss, and pull back.

Teaching: (i) this whole phrase can be repeated three or four times, slowing down and settling low in the last performance.

8 a,b Jumping and travelling

(ii) for the pull-back, the children move backwards slowly and strongly to show the force of the water.

3 'Can you turn as you pull back, swirling or drifting?'

Teaching: The children, while turning, should use less strength to emphasise the sensation of swirling or drifting. The whole phrase can be repeated about three or four times by the children individually.

Dance form

The children form small groups. Each group explores the idea of dancing part of the phrase in unison—perhaps until the tossing which splits up the group. Then it re-forms in the swirling, drifting, pulling back, only to break up yet again.

At the end, the children perhaps do not pull together in unison but may instead individually toss and toss and toss then swirl and drift off on their own, simulating the return to calmness.

Teaching: The children may choose to accompany the initial unison part with a tambourine played by one of the group, and then to pick up the accompaniment with their own voice sounds.

LESSON

Moon Landing

Accompaniment: *Electronic Movements* (see page 86).

The dance uses two parts of the record:

A is accompanied by the section *vibration*;

B is accompanied by the section *drifting*.

This dance concentrates on relationships and dynamics since its main movement ideas are *group rhythm* and contrasting qualities of *strength and lightness* and *speed and slowness*. The prior thinking required to translate the theme into movement experiences is not discussed here, since this lesson is intended for an older class of children and so assumes movement ability and understanding appropriate to such an age group.

62

Rhythmical introduction

The children experiment with sharp, angular, machine-like movements of the arms, legs, body and head. Each movement is isolated to a particular part of the body and so the effect is jerky and disjointed.

Teaching: The accompaniment of *vibration* helps the children to form rhythmical phrases.

Movement experiences

1 The class is given time to form a short, repeatable phrase from these isolated movements so that by repeating it the monotony of a machine-like rhythm may be experienced.

   Teaching: (i) the children may begin to incorporate stepping and turning into their movement patterns.
   (ii) again, music can assist the rhythmical phrasing and it should be played at regular intervals while the children are perfecting their pieces.

2 Each child having 'produced' a machine, the children can now work in groups of five to evolve a group machine on the same principle.

   Teaching: (i) the children may need some help with the concept of a group rhythm, or machine, in which each individual contributes only a small part of the whole. One plan is for each child to activate the person next to him in the group so that the entire group gradually becomes active, works as a whole, then the process is reversed till each child is motionless. Alternatively, one member of the group causes the rest to move and when this 'part' stops so the 'machine' comes to a stop also.
   (ii) the group sequence should be short and easily repeated.
   (iii) the children should decide which part of the moon vehicle their group sequence represents.

3 The children may now explore the possibilities of travelling and turning. They can speed up their turning until they are spinning fast, as 'magnetic fields' attract or repel them.

   Teaching: (i) this may represent a journey through space.
   (ii) the accompaniment may be played on the cymbal or

the record-section entitled *drifting* could be used.

4 Now let the children travel about, stepping extremely
slowly, lightly and as though pulled upwards, in order
to simulate the loss of gravitational pull and the resultant
weightlessness.

Teaching: To produce a rhythmical phrase, the children
should take three slow steps then try to bring the feet
together with an exaggeratedly slow gesture of the free
leg. When the feet come together the children begin to
bounce slowly on the spot.

5 The children may enjoy jumping and attempting to almost
float down again. This will be a new sensation for them.

Teaching: These jumps should not be vigorous, high jumps
but the time spent in the air should be as long as possible.

Dance form

The dance may be in two parts, depicting:

A the machine and its journey through space, accompanied
by *vibration* on the record;

B the 'moon walk', accompanied by *drifting*.

The children ought now to have sufficient movement
experience to be able to create their own 'moon landing'
dance. They should work in groups of four or five and the
class should all work together on part A before going on to
part B. This enables the teacher to provide the accompaniment
for all, and to some extent, to control the development of the
lesson in this way. She should move from group to group
and at intervals announce that the music will be played
and that all the groups will show what they have produced
up to that point in time. This gives her an opportunity to
see the various stages.

Words and sound

A further stimulus for expressive movement lessons is found
in the work that the children are doing in the classroom.
Many ideas that can be explored in movement come from
here. One very rich area is that of words. Children are learning
to appreciate the meaning of words and if they can select

'moving' words and can literally experience them in movement, they will have enriched their understanding of the meanings and will have added considerably to their expressive potential in movement.

The following is a sample of such words:

Stepping	Jumping	Turning
creeping	bouncing	whirling
stalking	leaping	revolving
marching	bounding	spinning
stamping	tossing	wheeling
	thrusting	
	flying	
	exploding	

Travelling	Stillness	Gesture
rushing	hesitating	crumpling
dashing	hovering	collapsing
darting	freezing	disintegrating
drifting	settling	
withdrawing		
retreating		

Each word has a dynamic element, e.g.
'whirling' may be translated by 'very quick turning',
'freezing' by 'strong stillness',
'drifting' by 'slow, gentle travelling' or even 'turning'.

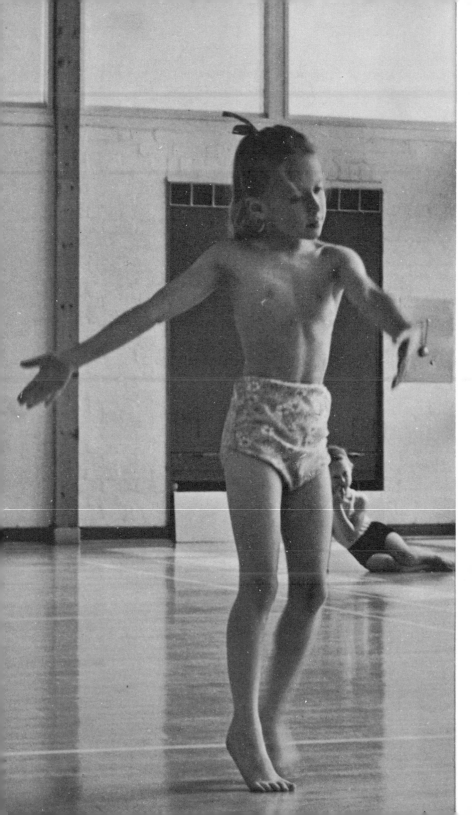

Selective use by the teacher of these and similar words throughout all expressive movement lessons can aid the children.
For example, if the children have been thinking of turning
quickly, the use of a word such as 'whirling' can make it
more meaningful for them.

When more than one word is combined to make a phrase,
some very interesting movement patterns begin to appear, e.g.
*darting and hovering—darting and hovering—wheeling—
settling.*

This might seem, for some children, to be what it feels like
to be a bird, and it may develop from here to become a dance
entitled *The Bird.*

A lesson based on words may take the following form :

Various words from the suggested lists are written on large
sheets of paper or on a frieze which can be displayed at the
lesson.

The 'jumping' words may be in *red* ;
the 'turning' words in *green* ;
the 'travelling' words in *blue,* and so on.

At the beginning of the lesson the children may choose one
word and experiment with movement interpretation. They
then try a second word, of a different colour this time. Next,
they may try out combinations of two words, and so on
until they reach the final form which might consist of one
word from each colour with perhaps two of one colour. This
ensures that the final form gives the children a balanced
variety of activities with contrasting dynamics. They may
need help with the sequence of the words and the linking
of one with another in movement. A clear starting situation
and a clear finish are very important in the final form.

This lesson is suitable for any stage in the children's experience. It is a very creative lesson : they can respond with
a wide variety of interpretations.

Music is an obvious source of ideas. When children listen
to a piece of music they may find themselves translating it
into movement terms very easily. 'That music makes me
think of . . . !' The dance which evolves may or may not use
the same piece of music as an accompaniment.

67

9 Drifting

The playing of percussion instruments may suggest certain movement responses which can be built into a dance form, the characteristics of each instrument and its sound giving variety and contrast (see p. 83ff).

Sound effects may also provide a source of ideas for expressive movement lessons. If children have a *Sound Table* in the classroom, many exciting sounds may be explored and some may be interpreted into movement ideas which could be further developed.

PART IV

**Stages of
development**

Development and progression

Within expressive movement, as in all subjects, there should be a recognisable development and progression in the children's ability and understanding. In order to achieve this, the teacher must demand standards and set goals. In any creative situation one tends to be wary of this in case the individual contribution is diminished or made more difficult, but these standards and goals are very important since it is only through mastery of material and subject matter that creativity can be so released that it finds its full expression.

(*a*) **an increase in physical skill**

This means a gradual mastery of their own bodies in movement and the ability to attempt increasingly difficult tasks. The children should gain satisfaction from achievement and thus be encouraged to do more, better.

(*b*) **a widening of the range of movement experiences**

When the child can say to himself, 'This is a new idea/ movement that I have not tried before', he has increased his vocabulary of movement and thus has greater resources in a creative situation.

(*c*) **a realising of creative potential**

As the children become more creative within the medium of movement they are able to respond more fluently to the teacher's questions and suggestions. They are also able to select movement phrases which are appropriate to what they wish to express.

The children must show some progress in all three areas if they are going to gain any satisfaction and benefit from expressive movement lessons. As they explore the creative possibilities, the children may set themselves a challenge which is beyond their physical ability at that moment. For a short time within the lesson therefore, they need help to acquire this physical skill before they can develop their initial ideas. As their physical skill increases so they find additional possibilities in movement, and thus build up a valuable store of experiences which support their creative attempts. The teacher must help them to realise that in all three areas there are standards at which they must aim.

Stages of development

The following three stages have been devised from observing the development of children's ability and understanding within each of the four aspects: namely, the *activities* which the children are able to master and enjoy, the *dynamics* of movement which they can experience and begin to control, the *space* around each child and the growing understanding of this concept, and the *relationships* for which the children have changing needs and which they are able to set up within their own movement world and between themselves and other people.

The contents of each stage are given only as a general guide. It is very difficult to predict when the children will pass from one stage to another, as the rate of development is different for each individual. Only the teacher can observe when the children have obviously progressed through one stage and are asking to be challenged within the next.

Stage I

Activities

(*a*) Large movements employing the whole body are natural at this stage.

(*b*) The main activities observed are turning, jumping and travelling.

(*c*) Stopping still is difficult but the child enjoys attempting it

Dynamics

(*a*) The child may have the ability to move very quickly or very slowly but may have little ability within these extremes.

(*b*) He enjoys his individual contribution to a class rhythm.

72

Space

(*a*) The child should appreciate the spatial extremes of high and low.

(*b*) He should be aware of different directions in movement but may show a tendency towards turning and moving forwards rather than backwards or to the side, since his 'space is all in front of him'.

Relationships

(*a*) These are between the class and the teacher in that the children move towards, away from and around her.

(*b*) The children are interested in moving by themselves and concentrate on their own movement only.

Stage II

Activities

The activities may now become physically more difficult, and the children show an increasing ability:

(*a*) to perform stepping and step-like movements which require greater balance;

(*b*) to combine activities, such as in turning jumps or travelling turns;

(*c*) to isolate movement to part of the body, as when one hand moves to meet the other hand to bring about a turn;

(*d*) to shape the body and to change this shaping, e.g. when sharp, linear shaping becomes rounded as the body turns;

(*e*) to balance on smaller areas of support;

(*f*) to produce asymmetrical movement.

Dynamics

Greater control of dynamics is shown in an ability:

(*a*) to become stronger/lighter/faster/slower;

(*b*) to appreciate the sensation of heaviness;

(*c*) to control speed;

(*d*) to appreciate gradually rhythmic phrase and pattern.

Space

The concept of space should be changing to include.

(*a*) an awareness of nearness to and distance from the body;

(*b*) a greater appreciation of direction in movement;

(*c*) an interest in, and understanding of, pathways on the floor.

Relationships

As there is no longer so much interest in self, relationship can be seen in:

(*a*) the enjoyment of working with a partner and imitating, copying and mirroring the other's movement;

,(*b*) an increasing ability to relate one part of the body to another part, as when trying to make one foot catch up with the other in the air while jumping or perhaps rolling over.

Stage III

Activities

It is at this stage that the child becomes very interested in his own ability and seeks mastery of his body in situations which require more skill. He now has the ability:

(*a*) to control the degree of turn while jumping and so can finish facing in the desired direction;

(*b*) to master the shaping of the body while in the air;

(*c*) to tumble and recover with ease;

(*d*) to have greater control of his feet, as when jumping off from two feet to land on only one.

74

Dynamics

He should have a greater range of dynamics at his disposal
in that he should be able:

(a) to experience movement which is extremely quick;

(b) to control his speed so that he can move with a steady,
slow motion;

(c) to attempt more complicated rhythms;

(d) to contribute to a group rhythm (for example, a group
rising and sinking movement demands an individual
awareness of the rhythmic pattern set up by the whole
group).

Space

His growing conception of space and of his place in it should
enable him:

(a) to be aware of the three dimensions of space;

(b) to trace clear pathways in the air around his body and
to repeat them, as may happen in a spiralling turn.

Relationships

As the child becomes more capable in movement, so he
should become more aware of others' movements and so
be able:

(a) to enjoy working on and contributing to a group idea;

(b) to be aware of more dramatic relationships in an action/
reaction situation with a partner, as when a strong
sharp movement towards a partner makes him recoil
and turn away;

(c) to contribute to situations in which interdependence is
essential, such as being responsible for much of his
partner's weight in lowering him slowly to the floor,
or by giving him the necessary counter-tension to balance
in an exciting situation and then to return from it;

(d) to relate one part of his body to another as he moves,
thus giving his movement more clarity and meaning.

75

Ideally, children starting school should begin at Stage 1 and should have passed through Stage 3 when they are ready to enter Secondary school. If a class in the later years of Primary school is having an expressive movement lesson for the first time, it is certainly not appropriate to begin at Stage 1. Children of this age require the challenge of Stage 3 but may not at first reach the required standard of ability, so it may be necessary to refer initially to certain activities in Stage 2. It may be helpful for the children to explore, for example, the shape of pathways on the floor (Stage 2) before attempting to shape pathways in the air (Stage 3).

10   *Steady, slow motion*

PART V
Accompaniment

Accompaniment

Dance may be accompanied or unaccompanied. Where there
is no recognisable accompaniment the silent rhythm of the
movement can be very satisfying to children. They can have
fun with a rich variety of sound accompaniments, which
include their own improvised voice sounds, words, phrases and
the reading of complete poems ; percussion instruments played
by themselves and/or the teacher ; their own music, or recorded
music which is chosen appropriately to support a particular
exploration in movement.

Children's voice sounds

Many voice sounds are not recognisable words but are the
product of the children's imagination. They very often discover
exciting rhythmical sounds, though these are usually effective
only when they are stimulated by the movement and so
develop with it and are an integral part of the whole experience. To require of the children that they produce a voice
sound to accompany their movement, if there is no indication
of a natural emergence of such a sound, could be to impose
an artificiality which would inhibit, rather than promote, rich
experience.

Descriptive, expressive words are fun for children as an
accompaniment to their movement, e.g. in a short dance based
on the trapping of one hand on the floor by the other : a
rhythmical pulling and sinking, pulling and sinking until one
last pull frees the hand and the whole body jumps into the
air to the joyous cry of 'I'm free !'.

A complete poem may be used as an accompaniment. The
rhythm, phrasing and meaning of the poem may match that
of the movement or dance almost exactly.

One good example is *Cat* by Eleanor Farjeon:

Cat
Scat
After her after her
Sleeky flatterer
Spitfire, chatterer
Scatter her, scatter her
Off her mat.
Wuff
Wuff
Treat her rough
Git her, git her
Whiskery spitter
Catch her, catch her
Green-eyed scratcher
Slathery
Slithery
Hisser
Don't miss her
Run till you're dithery
Hithery
Thithery
Pfitts, pfitts
How she spits
Spitch, spatch
Can't she scratch
Scritching the bark
of the sycamore tree
She's reached her arc
and hissing at me.
Pfitts, pfitts
Wuff wuff
Scat
Cat
That's
That.

This could be read aloud by the teacher, one child, or a group
of children, while another individual or group explores the
movement possibilities, forming a dance.
Unfortunately poems of such suitable form and content are
not very easy to find.

The dynamics of the overall rhythmical form—sudden and
slow movements, smoothness alternating with sharpness—

82

should be heard in the words, and seen and felt in the movement. Each should complement the other. In this way the poem
is at the same time stimulus and accompaniment to the dance.

Percussion

The instruments

Percussion instruments provide a rich source of accompaniment;
for example, one can use:

> tambour
> drums of various sizes
> tambourine
> cymbal
> Indian bells
> wooden blocks/wooden sticks
> castanets
> triangle
> shakers (maracas)

The playing of the instruments

Since these instruments are light and easy to carry, the children
may move and play simultaneously, providing a spontaneous
accompaniment for individual or group dance. At first this
may appear to inhibit some children's full participation in
movement, but if they can be encouraged to play the instrument
within the flow, timing and shape of the movement, then a
successful blending will develop. The children may accompany
each other, one playing for another or for a group, or, where
possible, a group may form a small percussion ensemble.
The latter requires more time to develop so that the group
accompaniment and the dance can confidently and success-
fully be combined.

The teacher may play the percussion instrument in order to
give the class a common movement experience. There are
two important features of this of which the teacher should
be particularly aware. She must play the instrument at a
tempo suited to children, which may be very different from
one suitable for adults. Also, she has here a very good
opportunity to lead the children into formed rhythmic
phrases.

The teacher and class should try to use as wide a variety of instruments as possible. Below are some suggestions for the playing of each instrument. The techniques involved are basically striking or shaking.

Tambour drums

These instruments are struck to produce clearly rhythmical beats and phrases. The pitch and sharpness of the sound varies depending upon whether the striking is performed by a soft-headed beater or a hard one, or by the hand or finger nail. Striking the skin with the hand, and the wooden rim with the stick of the beater, produces an interesting contrast in pitch which is helpful for a rhythmical stepping movement of dēep, hǐgh, hǐgh, hǐgh, dēep, hǐgh, hǐgh, hǐgh. The skin may also be 'smoothed around' with the palm or fingers; this produces a slow, continuous sound which is suited to turning carefully.

Tambourine

This instrument may be played by striking or by shaking and so it is a versatile instrument, producing contrasting sounds. The beating rhythms have an echo of the sound of the metal discs, which gives the beating a light quality. This is a good instrument to use for stepping phrases which accelerate into rapid travelling or turning.

Cymbal

This is an exciting instrument which can produce sound which accelerates and decelerates, and which increases and decreases in intensity. It is particularly apt for turning movements because of its continuous sound. If a staccato effect is wished, the sound is quickly cut off by striking the instrument and immediately gripping the edge.

Indian bells

The sound produced by this little instrument is very delicate and light and of a high pitch. It lasts for a long time and so can accompany a movement suspended in the air. Some young children are enraptured by this sensation. The bells are played by gently striking one against the other and if they are then drawn apart the sound seems to expand and follow them.

Wooden blocks/wooden sticks/castanets

The sound here is staccato and lively and asks to be formed into gay, rhythmic patterns for lively feet to dance to.
The wooden sticks or claves give their best sound if one of the sticks is laid along the fingers of a lightly closed fist and the other stick strikes it sharply.

Triangle

The shape of the triangle means that it can produce a single sound if struck on one side only, or if the beater strikes all sides in rapid succession then a more restless rhythm is produced which may accompany turning.

Shakers

It is to this group that the children can contribute many of the instruments that they themselves make. They can experiment with containers and contents and will discover a variety of sounds. Metal bottle tops nailed to sticks also produce interesting sounds.

If the percussionist, when playing, copies the quality and shape of the dancers' movement, then the sound will be right for the movement. In other words, the hand or the beater should move on the instrument as the children move on the floor. For example, if the children are bouncing off the floor, the percussionist's hand should also bounce off the skin rather than hit into the instrument; if a heavy, collapsing fall is being accompanied, then the hand should fall heavily on to the skin of the tambour or drum; if the children are rising gently and sinking a little, rising again and so on, then the Indian bells should rise and sink with the movement; if the movement phrase necessitates travelling or turning, then the instrument should not be held still as the sound is produced but should be moved around to project the sound.

Music

Very little music which has not been written or adapted for
children's dance is truly suitable for accompaniment.
Musical pieces are generally too long and rhythmically un-
suitable for children.
Some pieces which *have* been arranged for young people
appear on the following records:

Listen, Move and Dance	Series 1-3	H.M.V. 7EG 8727/8/9
Listen and Move	Series 1-8	MacDonald and Evans
Tunes for Children		E.M.I.
Stories in Movement	Series 1-4	E.M.I. 7EG 8976/7/8/9
Electronic Movements	(by Tom Dissevelt)	Philips 430 736 PE

Suggestions for the use of these particular pieces are given
with most of the records, but the teacher should feel free to
use the music for other movement ideas. The children may
contribute music which has a particular appeal to them but
care should be taken to see that any piece which they wish
to dance to is short and well phrased.

PART VI

**Links with
other subjects**

There are certain aspects of expressive movement which are shared with other subjects. Three of these—rhythm, shape and mood—are outlined here. An understanding of these aspects in more than one subject gives the children a much fuller appreciation of their significance. If the teacher draws the children's attention to the common features as they meet them in such subjects as literature (both prose and poetry), art, music, and mathematics, then the children's learning will be more comprehensive and their ease in relating these features will be increased.

Rhythm

An understanding of the nature of rhythm and its effect on movement can be developed in children if they are encouraged to build rhythmical patterns as they move and to enjoy the natural rhythm of each movement. Children enjoy repetition and will be absorbed by this sensation for some time, but they need help to round off a series of repetitions so that they form a rhythmical phrase. For example, a child will *turn—turn—turn—turn. . . .* Suggest that he tries to *turn and freeze,* or *turn and settle,* and so makes the movement pattern *turn—turn—turn—turn and settle.*

For each child a turn has its own rhythmical property and a completed phrase its own dynamic structure. An appreciation of rhythm and of a formed pattern can be developed, as mentioned above, in the children's work in poetry, prose, mathematics, music and art. In these the rhythmic structure of the words, numbers or sounds is important, and if a child has *read* rhythmically, *heard* rhythm and also *experienced* it in body movement, then his appreciation will be so much more complete. The reader is referred to the children's poems which follow later in this part.

Shape

Children become aware of shape in many ways. They learn
to recognise spatial relationships and how to determine the
shaping of the natural and man-made objects with which they
are familiar. How much better will they understand shaping
if they have felt this as a living, moving reality in their own
bodies? As they spread their bodies wide, so they feel the
flatness of this movement. If they twist their bodies they
appreciate the rounded, tortuous shaping which is emerging.
By narrowing all their attention both mentally and physically
upon one focal point, they know how arrow-slim shaping is
achieved.

As they swing through changing curves, twists, arcs and
circles, as they bounce and shoot in and out of sharp angles
and up and down lines in space, so the children will appreciate
more fully such spatial shapings and will proceed with more
ease to reproduce them on paper or in three-dimensional
work. Thus expressive movement helps them to form a concept
of shape.
Movements like these also have rhythmic phrasing which adds
to the children's appreciation of the rhythm in their environment.

Mood

Movement is a means of expressing mood. Jumping may show
frustration, anger or joy, each jump being different from the
others. Movement with a downward stress may suggest sad-
ness while upward movement may be an expression of light-
heartedness.
Movement will also *bring about* changes of mood. Turning
gently, with a closing of the body, may induce a solemn
calm mood, while a gay period of jumping with a clear
rhythmical pulse may produce a mood of brightness and
liveliness.

Awareness of mood and of how it can be induced and expressed
may also be explored in music, poetry and prose. The power
of sound, words and movement to invoke and express varying

moods is very real to children. They come to realise that mood
resulting from involvement in one medium may be expressed
through another. Here, for example, is a poem inspired by
listening to music:

> It makes you feel happy and lively
> And you think of horses too,
> You twirl and twirl untill your dizzy
> But the music always keeps busy
> Untill it gets slower and slower
> But even louder still
> Then you think of thunder beside a hill.
>
> Georgette Robb
> Age 9

Integrated experiences

The following poems, which show an awareness of movement,
present an interesting contrast. In the first, the writer has
observed movement in a bird, movement which is *external*
to himself but much of which he is experiencing *within*
himself. In the second, first-hand experience is being
expressed: the joy of singing, laughing, shouting and dancing,
and the ultimate freedom that this writer feels, may indeed
be in the 'twirling wind rushing through the trees and grass'.

> A hawk on the wing
> Gliding and swooping around and about
> It makes you want to sing
> Up and down and round and round
> It never seems to touch the ground.
>
> Weightless in the air
> And down it comes to frighten a hare
> Up and out of bounds
> Down to the mounds
> Squawks to a postman on his rounds.
>
> Ian Williamson
> Age 9

92

The Music

I want to sing and laugh and shout
And do many other things
It makes me think of twirling wind
Rushing through the trees and grass.
To dance and dance and dance and dance
Right through its lovely tone.

Alison Dutch
Age 9

There exists a very close link between music and dance.
Something very exciting is achieved when the children can
compose their own music and then dance to it or when they
have a dance idea which they are exploring and they make
their own accompaniment.

A very successful and satisfying sharing of music and dance
is possible where the children are familiar with the creative
approach to music-making, as outlined by Carl Orff in his
work for children which is known as *Orff Schulwerk.*

These situations, in which one experience stimulates another,
should arise as naturally as possible and should not be forced
or contrived. However, the teacher can make it possible for
each child to pursue the links as he sees them and as he is
motivated by each different experience. For instance, when
one medium proves inadequate for producing what the child
wants, he may perhaps complete his work by pursuing the
idea into another medium. He may find his present vocabulary
inadequate to describe an idea and so may enter the realm
of movement to satisfy his need.

'. . . children should be provided with rich learning opportunities
from an early age rather than be required to attain high standards of
specific performance *at* an early age.'*

*The Psychology of Learning, R. Borger and A. E. M. Seaborne (Penguin), p. 103.

93

Bibliography

Childhood and Movement, D. Jordan. Blackwell
Modern Educational Dance, R. Laban. MacDonald and Evans
Creative Dance in the Primary School, J. Russell. MacDonald and Evans
Modern Dance in Education, J. Russell. MacDonald and Evans

Also in this series:

Inventive Movement

Margaret E. Anderson

Inventive movement is concerned with the management of the body in meeting progressively demanding challenges and problems. It is concerned with agility of mind in thinking round the problems and with agility of body in solving them. Primary school children have abounding energy. Their enthusiasm for moving, climbing and scrambling can be harnessed to well-planned and purposeful inventive movement lessons.

It is the aim of this book to give help and guidance to the Primary school teacher so that her lessons will allow her pupils, whatever their age and their stage of development, to become skilful in the management of their own bodies, thus giving satisfaction and joy which lead to self-confidence and poise.

Games Skills

Margaret E. Anderson

Games skills lessons must be thought out and planned to ensure progression. Too often has the time allocated to games been spent in running team races which afford no real challenge and certainly no progression in the acquisition of skill.

This book identifies the objectives in teaching games skills and games to Primary school pupils, outlines the general principles of lesson planning, and contains suggestions for a variety of skills practices and games. Teachers who widen the opportunities for their pupils in the games skills aspect of Physical Education will quickly discover that children gain much enjoyment and satisfaction from skills practices in themselves and that many reach a standard which neither they nor their teacher had realised was possible.